NEVER ALONE

by Michelle Irene

First Edition
Edited by Sarah Delarco
May 2015

Revised Edition
July 2015

DEDICATION

To my Mom and Dad
for teaching me about love, faith and Angels.

To my amazing children Derek and Taylor
my inspiration for being .

To my wonderful husband Todd to whom I could never have
accomplished all that I have with out his continuous support,
encouragement, and most of all, love.

ACKNOWLEDGMENTS

If we were all like angels, the world would be a heavenly place. ~Author Unknown

I am blessed.

I thank the good Lord everyday for the abundances I have received and the wonderful life I live. While getting up close and personal with all who have so kindly shared their amazing moments of Angels with me, I have found that my life has become even more enriched than before. I have had the opportunity to meet so many wonderful people who opened their hearts to me and shared some very personal moments. I am forever grateful to them for their contributions. I am so excited to now be able to share these stories with you in hopes to enrich your life, if even for a moment you feel the touch of an Angel.

*some of the names in the stories have been changed to protect the privacy of those involved.

CONTENTS

	Acknowledgments	4
1	I Believe	7
2	Inspiration from Heaven	11
3	I Need A Sign	27
4	Scent of An Angel	33
5	The Power of Money	39
6	Birds of A Feather	45
7	I'm A Dreamer	53
8	Do You Hear What I Hear	61
9	Light Up My Life	67
10	Earth Angels	77
11	Saving Grace	83
12	Simple Reminders	87
13	Children and Angels	95
14	Build It and They Will Come	99
	About The Author	107

Chapter 1
I BELIEVE

I saw the angel in the marble and carved until I set him free. ~Michelangelo

I believe. I always have and I always will. For as long as I can remember Angels have always been a part of my life.

A fond first time memory is observing the painted Angels similar to a Michelangelo Masterpiece on the ceilings of our local Catholic Church, St. Joseph's in Endicott NY. During the weekly mass we would attend, I would stare into the eyes of the angelic individuals, feeling as if I knew them - seeing right into their souls and feeling as if they were communicating with me but I wasn't sure what they were saying. I was amazed by their beauty, their strength and purity. I was Intrigued to say the least. Maybe it was because I often asked my Mother, "How come I wasn't at your wedding with you and Daddy?" and her response was always the same - "because you were playing with the Angels – you weren't born yet." And so the intrigue continued, and I believe I really was playing with the Angels.

Are we really just an energy source like many others have suggested? I don't know and I'm not here to prove or disprove this theory. What I can tell you are my thoughts and my experiences. I belicve that we are all made of energy and everything surrounding us is a form of energy. We transmit energy vibrations, and we receive energy vibrations. What we think, feel, wish for is sending a signal out into the universe. Somewhere out there it reflects and comes back to us.

Heaven is right above us almost as if we could touch it, like a different frequency similar to that of the radio and satellites. Before we are born, we are energy. While here on this earth, we are energy. And when we pass on to the after-life, we are still energy. Our bodies here on earth are just a shell for us to live our life and to meet our worldly goals. When we pass, our soul, which is made of energy, travels through the frequency with all other energies. See the pattern? I want to share with you my experiences and to share the experiences of others in their own words of how, for only a moment in time, they were touched, encouraged, or directed by a greater power I call Angels.

What is an Angel?

"Are not all angels ministering spirits sent to serve those who will inherit salvation?" Hebrews 1:14, NIV

There are so many books and websites out there with definitions of what their interpretation of an angel is or isn't. Some say there are three different types of angels and some say there are thousands with individual names. My plan is not to go there because honestly, I'm not an Angel expert. If you would like to learn more about the assortment of angelic realms you can easily find your answers by asking our good friends, Google or Amazon, for a great array of books, websites, and blogs to choose from. There are many definitions and variations in today's society and we may really never know the true meaning.

All we have is what we read, what we hear, and what our own experiences may be. The translation is up to the individual. The following are some definitions that you can use as a guideline if you wish. The Google definition of an Angel is as follows:

Angel : /anjel/noun
1. a spiritual being believed to act as an attendant, agent, or messenger of God, conventionally represented in human form with wings
2. an attendant or guardian spirit

The word angel is derived from the Latin word angelus meaning "messenger". We may refer to our experiences as being with our Guardian Angels. Some believe our loved one's who have passed cannot be a guardian angel. I think differently. It all depends on what your definition is , what you have learned or have been taught and what you believe.

Dictionary.com and the British Dictionary say

Guardian Angel : noun
1. an angel believed to watch and protect someone
2. a helpful or protective person

Then there is the terminology used often – Spirit Guide. We are all assigned Spirit Guides who help us through life. They guide us through good times and in bad but can not tell us what to do. The choice's are essentially up to us. They are angelic, and therefore to me, are a form of an Angel.

Wikipedia.org describes a Spirit Guide as such

Spirit Guide:
                   A term used by Western Tradition to describe an

entity that remains a dis-incarnate spirit in order to act as a guide, a protector to a living incarnate human being.

You can see where the confusion can come into play. If you look closely you will see all three have a common ground – to GUIDE, GUARD, and PROTECT. That's all I need to know. Can you detect which is which when you have an angelic moment? Probably not for most of us. I think all you need to know is that someone up above is here to help you, to guide you and to protect you. Our loved ones who have passed are like angels now, and they live as spirits in Heaven with God, which to me, is a form of an Angel. They are all Angels in my book and in my life.

It's not about the terminology, but about the experience and how it helps us here on Earth to guide us through this wonderful journey we call life.

If you believe, and chances are you probably do (or you wouldn't be reading this), then I know you will truly enjoy the experiences that have been shared by many that follow. The stories are not about large miraculous events, but rather small moments, meaningful moments, heartwarming moments.

If you are a non-believer or a skeptic in the higher frequency of energy and you are curious, then I sincerely hope you read every story and come out at the end a believer.

Either way, my desire is that you come along on this amazing journey and enjoy these occurrences, big or small, but none the less amazingly beautiful—it is so comforting to see that when you are touched by an Angel you are Never Alone.

Chapter 2
INSPIRATION FROM HEAVEN

The guardian angels of life fly so high as to be beyond our sight, but they are always looking down upon us. ~Jean Paul Richter

If I'm not a medium, a psychic or an expert at all in the field of spiritualism and the other side then why write a book? I mean seriously, what gives me the right?

Would it surprise you if I told you my Angels expressed to me to "Write the book?" LOL I know right? Exactly what I was thinking. Well they did, numerous times, throughout the past 10 years, and I have been guided to this point in time where I sit at my computer sharing the stories that have been brought to me through my angels and through other people as well.

Many years ago when I first starting designing handbags – yes I am a handbag/accessory designer – I would hand sew a small brass angel on every bag I created. This was a symbol that, for some reason, I felt compelled to share with everyone who chose to purchase one of my bags. I wanted to get the word out. The hang tag on the bags explained why I attached this angel figure and its importance. "This angel is a symbol to remind you, you are never alone, someone is always with you watching over you."

I had surrounded myself and our home with angels. There was

an angel strategically placed in every room of our house for protection and a gentle reminder that there is a greater force, a greater energy protecting us at all times. I had experienced a few encounters with angels which were the true inspiration behind this symbolism. One of my most memorable stories was a night that I saw a full embodied spiritual being.

An Angel in my Room

It was like any other evening, the kids were in bed, sound asleep in the bedroom next to ours. Nothing out of the ordinary had happened that day or evening. My husband, Todd and I went to bed like any other night. I was awakened in the middle of the night when I felt as if someone was watching us. I opened my eyes to look in the doorway thinking it would be my son, Derek, who had this habit of waking in the night and would come to our room and stop in our doorway without saying a word, which always scared the bajeebers (very professional word) out of me. I did not see him there. I continued to look over to Todd's side of the bed because I still felt a presence in the room. And there it was much to my surprise, I saw a boy standing near our window and I remember the vision as clear as day. He was not human – he was transparent. I could see right through him yet his shape and face were so full of detail. He had a red baseball cap on and had one arm resting on the window sill just watching over us. Of course, being the first time I really remember ever seeing an apparition, I was a little freaked out!

I quickly looked away and closed my eyes but had to take another peak...he was gone. Glad, sad, and terrified, I really didn't know what to make of this experience. Little did I know he was sending me a message, but it took a few months before I truly understood what that message was.

The next morning I called my Dad because I knew he would be able to answer my questions of what I saw. "Dad, what is the difference between a ghost, a spirit, and an angel," I said excitedly. Of course many questions were asked to why I was on a quest for information on this subject, so I told him of the experience I had the night before.

The most profound question he had me consider was if "Did this sighting felt threatening or scary in any way?" My response was "no, he was very calm, almost like he was protecting us or someone. I can't quite explain it."

Months had gone by and no more sightings of my young man visitor.

Meanwhile, we had moved to a new home and my son Derek had met a new friend. They met on the school bus and also attended Religious Instructions together at the church we attended regularly. The two had hit it off famously and were sure to be best buddies for a while.

Like any good parent, you want to be able to meet the parents of the child that your children play with. The boys wanted to get together after school hours and so it was time to meet the parents of his new found friend. We walked around the block to their home and knocked on the door. When the door opened we were greeted with such warmth and love I knew this was going to be the start of something beautiful.

Derek and I stepped into the living room and there it was! The picture on the wall ….I recognized this young man...he was the angel I saw in our bedroom at our other house!!! OMG, I can only imagine the look I had on my face especially once I found out that this young man, our new friend's son, Paul, aka PJ, had passed away in a tragic car accident a few months before.

As I looked around the room I noticed a trunk which happened to be set up as a memorial for PJ and placed on the ledge of this antique trunk was a red baseball cap. The red baseball cap he was wearing when he appeared in my previous home in Hillcrest. I then realized my recollection was correct and this was the young man that had come to me and brought me to his home to become a good friend for his mother, Sue.

Of course it was many years before I even mentioned my experience to Sue. Talking about angels and spirits was still a bit of a hush hush thing because people would think you were weird or crazy, but when I finally did about seven years later we both broke down in tears with the realization of the gift of friendship that her eldest son PJ had given to us.

He was watching over his Mom and guided our family to our new home in Chenango Forks so that she would never be alone. To this day we are still the best of friends.

So angels can bring you together with people who need you or who you may need for friendship, love, healing, or guidance because they are always with you watching over you and protecting you.

It was during this same time period before we moved to the new house in Chenango Forks just mentioned that another divine intervention had taken place. Whose hand was in the vessel? Was it PJ again? Was this all part of the divine plan? You decide.

It wasn't until writing these words on paper did I come to realize that maybe?

To Move or Not To Move?

The house in Hillcrest which we were currently residing in was of good size. It was a 3-bedroom house, but 2 bedrooms were on the 3rd level and 1 bedroom on the main level. We have 2 children, Taylor, our beautiful daughter is the youngest and Derek our amazing son, is the oldest. They shared a room for the first few years because it was just easier having them both right next door to our bedroom.

Then that appropriate age seemed to be nearing where it was time to split them up, especially being different sexes. Todd and I had made the decision to relocate Derek's room to the main level to give him his own space and privacy. The room really was not big enough to be used as a master bedroom so it seemed to be the better choice. We really pumped up the move to the new room with excitement, "new comforter set with matching window treatments, paint colors and even a new family pet ... Rocky the turtle. Bribery will get you everywhere. Not really. We even installed an intercom system so Derek could talk to us in the middle of the night if need be, but this wouldn't work either.

He could not stay in the room by himself. (Little did he know that a previous owner had actually passed away in that room and I know he could sense his presence). Although there were never any paranormal activities with this knowledge my husband and I both had of the past we could definitely sense the presence of an undetermined energy .

We decided to look into renovating our home and compare the

cost of an addition to moving to a new home. After seeing the price of renovating we chose the later and started looking for a new home.

I diligently searched the paper every Sunday (the internet listings of homes for sale were not yet available and you still had to go directly to the real estate agent for information).

This one house always seemed to appear and 'pop' out at me. I really liked it but the cost was way more then we could afford, but week after week it continued to be listed as the price slowly started to lower. I remember saying a prayer. "Lord if this is the house we are supposed to have then we need a little help."

Another month or so went by and the price had dropped drastically and there happened to be an open house. So we decided what the heck---let's check it out. The moment we walked in we knew it was our home but the sale price was still more than we could afford.

As we were leaving the house, the realtor mentioned that the owners were in a hurry to sell (they were already living out of town and the house was empty) and he said "just throw a crazy price out there—they might bite." Well we threw the crazy price out there and they bit – however we were still $8,000 dollars short for closing costs and didn't know if we were going to be able to close the deal. The house may just slip away from us. I went into prayer mode again. "Lord you brought us to this house for a reason, and we are still short the amount we need to close on the deal. Can you please give us a sign or assistance if this is to be our next move?"

At the time, my husband, Todd was very interested in the stock market and dabbled at investing and decided that morning to purchase a stock for a short sale and lo and be hold by the close of the market that very same day can you guess the amount that he had earned off that stock? Yup.................... $8,100...almost the exact amount we needed to purchase the house.

NOTE: (this is the house that we moved into that was located around the corner from PJ's house where I met Sue, after I saw his spirit in our Hillcrest bedroom.)

Was it PJ helping our angels and spirit guides make it happen? After all if we didn't move to the new location in Chenango Forks, Sue and I probably wouldn't have met.

Sometimes when we ask for help or guidance it doesn't always happen in one big swoop. It may be in phases, placing people in our lives at moments they are needed, or being placed in someone's life when they need you.

Many want or expect results/answers right away and in reality it takes time, like many other things in life. Did you learn to walk the first time you stood up? Did you stay on your bicycle the first time you peddled on your own? I think you get my point. Patience is a wonderful virtue and usually is worth the wait.

These are a few of the stories that have inspired me to share and to talk with others in search of similar messages, occurrences, and experiences – everyday people and the Angels helping us in our daily lives. The stories may not be large miraculous events. They come to us every day in many different ways and the way for me to share these narrations would be in a book, when the time was right. I felt a bit hesitant about writing on this topic. What would it do to my reputation, my family's reputation? People can be cruel and ridicule and so I felt the timing was just not right. Book on hold.

Enter the picture 7 years later as my Angels so kindly remind me of what my new venture is to be. This is the experience that has propelled me in the direction of which I am now sitting at my laptop pounding away at the keyboard keys not quite fast enough for my fingers to keep up while I excitedly note all the amazing moments I have had with my angels.

Write the Book

While on a trip to Florida – it was a rainy day and we decided to head on over to the local book store. Taylor was taking on-line classes during college break to collect more credits so that she could graduate college early. I was working on my business at my laptop because of the free internet that was supplied by the store and felt the urge to walk around the store to browse.

 I found myself over at the new age section which I hadn't visited in many years and was contemplating on purchasing some tarot cards. I had been thinking about teaching myself how to read them and use them in my daily life for inspiration.

And that's when I heard it......."Write the Book." It was so loud and clear, and I looked around me to see who was talking to me or who was near me having a conversation. No one in sight. Wait--What? Did I just hear someone say "Write the Book?" And so the thought process began.

Am I hearing right, did I really hear that? Which book are they talking about (I had a few options in my years of ideas for different books). So I let it go.

It was only a few days later still in Florida when this next visitation took place but I would not immediately understand it's true purpose....

Sky Angels

I'm not a morning person and my entire family knows this. I love staying up late and enjoy my moments of solitude and quietness. However one morning, while on a vacation in Florida, I awoke before anyone and quietly slipped out of bed (With any movement I usually wake my husband when I ever so rarely do wake before him so I was surprised he didn't move an inch) and decided to sit out on the patio facing out to the ocean for a speculator view of the morning sunrise. This morning was to become a very special moment as I found such beauty in this particular sunrise.

The colors and the calmness of the ocean waves were soothing to the soul. I felt such peace and love. For some reason I decided to get my cell phone to take a photo of this gift from the heavens. I have always felt inspiration from what I call 'sky angels'.

Sky Angels are those moments when I see a breathtaking image in the clouds creating unique shapes, the lights shining through the clouds creating a light show with its rays projecting through, a rainbow and it's ever amazing color schemes so vibrant.

Only a handful of times have I observed these moments when for some unknown reason I am aware--as if they were a gift from a loved one passed, a moment in time to send their love and say hello. It's not an ongoing thing – it happens on rare occasions. It's not every ray of light or every rainbow you see, it's a moment, a feeling, a knowing.

I took the picture, okay I took about five, and rested on the swinging love seat in solitude capturing this beautiful moment in my mind and feeling loved. It wasn't until later when I really took a good look at the picture did I discover that above the sun the clouds had formed into a pair of what appeared to be angel wings and the reflection from the sun on the ocean was in the form of the Cross!! Two definite signs that were a gift from above........

A few weeks later I was showing my mother in law, Nancy the picture and she pointed out that the sun was in the shape of a heart and the clouds surrounding the sun and the reflection looked like another set of angel wings. WOW !!!

Why would this entice me to write a book you ask? Well of course, there is more to the story in regards to this situation and the voice saying "write the book." Remember I said that sometimes messages are brought to us in parts. Maybe to understand them completely because we are not always aware when they try to capture our attention. I mean after all I did shake off the loud "Write the Book" voice I heard.

Two days after my return to New York from our Florida vacation I was about to embark on an experience I would never forget. I was going to be on the set for an upcoming new television series on the network TLC called "Angels Among Us" starring Rosie

Cepero. Yes a show about Angels! Still not the moment I decided to write this book. Hold on, it's coming soon...It is always amazing to me how the spirit world works. Coincidence? I think not. I don't believe in coincidence....I believe God puts people, places, and things into our lives at strategic moments whether it's for a minute or many, many years. It's up to us to notice these moments of opportunities and blessings then decide why they were given to us and what we are to take away from them. Comfort, peace, love, awareness, or is it a message to do good for others?

Rosie is a medium and an exceptional one at that and as part of her new series she would have guests come to her beautiful log cabin in a nearby town to receive messages from their angels. When I first stepped into her home, I could feel the love and warmth that embraced the property. This was a special place to be. A moment in time to savor. Now most people would be so excited about being on television. Me? I couldn't wait to have a reading and receive messages from my loved ones passed. The TV thing was cool but not my main excitement. I'd had a handful of readings before from other mediums and psychics and the outcome has always been fulfilling. With feelings of love and peacefulness the moment I met Rosie, I knew this would be a powerful moment in my life!

If you haven't watched the show yet – look it up – I promise you will be amazed and fall in love with this exceptionally talented woman. Rosie greeted me with the warmest, most sincere hug and looked at me and said "Oh this is going to be good. You have amazing positive energy and are surrounded by many angels."

Sometimes when people arrive for a reading they are nervous

because they don't know what to expect or are hesitant on the messages they might receive, but I was ready to go.

Once all the release papers were signed and the cameras were ready to roll we began our reading:

A Reading from Rosie

I'm not a skeptic when it comes to medium ship however with cameras there and this being a television show, I wasn't quite sure what to expect. I had decided to make sure I did not show much emotion and give away any details of what she may have been receiving from my loved ones. I wanted to make sure this was authentic for myself, for the show, and for Rosie. "Violet, a violet color coming through" says Rosie, "what is the significance of this color?" Hah, this is my favorite color and the signature color of the interior of my handbag collection. OK off to a good start.

"A dark haired women coming through for you....your Mother....she's fine. No more cancer." (yes she passed from cancer).

"She's showing me a red Campbell soup can, did she drink Campbell soup, did she have chicken noodle soup?" Oh wow I think as I take a long deep breath not really sure how to respond. I then clarify the connection for Rosie and explain that I would smell my mother's homemade chicken noodle soup at random times and just knew that it was her stopping by to say hello.

"There's a man, a sort of chubby guy (yes my Dad was a chubby jolly fellow) coming through....they have a connection....Pop, Father, it's your Dad. Your Mom and Dad are here. Embrace it."

OK OK , give me proof is what I was thinking. Rosie continues with the reading and proceeds to tell me " I keep hearing Joe" OKAY WOWZA. The night before I had stumbled upon my father's hospital bracelets in one of my desk drawers . I placed them inside my handbag (yes it was a Michelle Irene Convertible Bag-product placement people, c'mon). It is one of those odd items that you feel the need to hang onto. I decided to put it in my bag because for some reason, dad was always a bit hesitant to come through or speak out at readings, and I really wanted to hear from him. So I reach into my bag to pull out the validation for Rosie that what she was hearing was true. This was my dad.

"You're dad is telling me there's a connection with you, him and the beach. Something about a sunrise."

OMG just a few days earlier was when I took the picture of the sunrise on the beach! This was him....with me at that moment. I get it! I get the love, the peacefulness I was feeling at that time. He was with me!!!

 Rosie continues on with more communications from my parents and at different times they asked about the book. Rosie inquires "are you writing a book?" I told her about all my thoughts from the past including the voice I had heard only a few days earlier "write the book" and she said this was validation that that is what you're suppose to do and the picture from your dad....that's the cover!

After working on the design for the cover because it was taken with my cell phone I just couldn't get it to look just right. I have included it in the photo section for you to see!

This is the picture I took one morning as
the sun rose in Florida. You can see the
angel wings in the clouds, the wings
coming off the sun, the sun heart shape and the reflection of the
sign of the Cross on the ocean water from the sun. I really wanted
to use this for the cover but because it was taken on my cell phone
the resolution was not strong enough to warrent being the cover
picture.

Get it now? Get the message? See how the spirit world can work in stages and guide you in directions you should go. I don't know if I would have ever decided to continue with this thought that I had had over seven years ago about writing a book to share inspirational stories of our Angels guiding us through our time on Earth. My Angels, however, knew differently.

Taylor and I with Rosie
from the TLC Show
"Angels Amoung Us"
at a special Fundraising
Event.

Chapter 3
I NEED A SIGN

For he will order his angels to protect you wherever you go. Psalm 91:11

How do you know? How do you know someone is with you? How do you know you're not alone? How do you know there is a greater world out there besides the one we are living here on Earth? What are the signs, what should you look for?

We all have the ability to hear, feel, or see our angels. We are born with this gift. It's a part of our being. Unfortunately somewhere along the line we have been instructed to shut it down… it's not real, it's just your imagination, people will think you're crazy and so on. That's what we are taught and eventually we lose the ability of our "Sixth Sense" so-to- speak.

However, like any other muscle in our body (not that it's a muscle don't mistake what I'm saying), it's a sense, a feeling, a knowing, and you can learn to use it again. The more you use it, the stronger it will become. If you don't use it, you lose it.

Repetition and patience are the way to go. You can't force them to come to you. Talk to your loved ones whenever you feel the need. You're not crazy, I promise, (at least in this situation – your other mental status-hmmm, not my business lol). Whether you speak to them in your mind or out loud, guess what? They hear you. The more you acknowledge them and talk to them the easier your communication with them will become.
Now I'm not saying you will become the next big psychic or a

medium. That's a really amazing gift to be blessed with but we can receive messages of love & encouragement from loved ones passed, our spirit guides, guardian angels or whatever you would like to cal them. We just have to learn to listen. Shut off all the chaos from our everyday life – relax – believe and really, really listen. When you ask, they may not answer immediately. They may not be ready or you may not be ready. The reason is unknown but they are there – remember? We are never alone.

This book is not about teaching you how to communicate with your angels or the after-life. I do not claim to be able to teach you how to talk with your loved ones who have passed, I can only tell you how I do it, and share what I have learned. What has worked best for me. Each person is different, and it's up to you to learn in your own way with your own signs. If you start to pay attention to the clues that are around you, you too may be able to share some amazing discoveries of communications or messages from loved ones on the other side. Angels have a special way of making themselves known. The following steps are how I have been able to make it work for me.

Step 1:The first thing you need to do is to just believe.

Step 2: Ask for protection from the white light. This is a very powerful protective shield provided by your guardians. It can protect you from negative energy, act as a healthy shield and protect you from whatever you may, but you have to ask for its protection.

Step 3: Ask for a sign. Below I share with you many signs that I have experienced that make me a believer. The more you pay attention the more signs you'll be able to recognize. If you do not understand and see any of the signs they are sending you, ask them to send some that you will better understand.

Step 4: Don't push it, don't try too hard. You can't make them appear. They come when they are ready, when you're ready, when the time is just right.

13 Signs that your Angels may be trying to communicate with YOU:

1. Fragrance – Have you ever noticed an aroma of sorts that reminds you immediately of someone you know?
2. Coins – Do you find pennies or other coins in odd places? Usually this is a sign from above. Hence the term "pennies from heaven."
3. Flying Friends – Have you ever had a visit from a Bird, a dragonfly, a butterfly?
4. Feeling – Sometimes you get a certain feeling when someone has joined you. I get this odd feeling in my chest like a heaviness, but it doesn't hurt. It's just different. Tingling and goosebumps are other forms of recognition.
5. Shadows – Have you ever seen something pass you by in your peripheral vision and you look, but nothing is there? This could be a sign.
6. Lights – Flickers, specks, and rooms filled with light
7. Call your Name – Have you ever heard your name being called out only to realize no one is around?
8. Dream Visitation – Have you ever received a message or a visit in your dreams and felt it was so real?
9. Object Movement – They are powerful enough to move objects in order to get your attention if it is really necessary.
10. Music & Other Electronics– Music, blinking lights, ceiling fans, stopping watches, draining batteries from tech devices, turning off or on a television are all signs that spirit is

around.

11. Temperature Change – Some people feel a sudden change in temperature-some cold some warm.

12. Time Slows Down – There have been instances where time has slowed down or even felt as if it has stopped if only for a moment during times of protection from your guardian angel.

13. Earth Angel – One moment they are here and the next they are gone. Or maybe you've met someone who is so special, so angelic, you just know that's there purpose.

These are just some examples of signs that you may be receiving a visit from your angels, your guardian angel or your spirit guide. There are many other ways that you can be contacted, just be aware.

Ask, Believe, Receive.

The next story is how I simply just asked a question and got my response. I believed my angels would answer me . So I asked, then waited for a response but I didn't have to wait long.

Third Time's A Charm

While the thought process began on what to name the title of my book, a few ideas came to mind. I had decided to go with Never Alone going back to the beginning of my Handbag Design Days with the hang tag message "You are never alone, someone is always with you watching over you." Never before have I written a book, so of course self doubt comes into play. Is this right? Will people understand?

I was on a flight home and thinking more about the book. How to set it up, will it make sense to people, how can I make it an easy read, how can I reach out and touch people, help them, and is the title right. So I turned to guidance from my Angels. "I need a sign that this is the right title." That is all I said and within minutes I had my response.

I was thumbing through a magazine – a Fashion Magazine and there it was – bright BOLD letters in the words 'Never Alone'. OK that's good Angels, not bad. For some reason I felt the need to not accept just one sign, I feel better when it was three. Why three? I really don't know maybe to reassure myself that I'm not making up the signs – looking too hard – maybe I'm just a perfectionist and want to make sure it's right.

A few hours later while reading a book, there it was again "Never Alone." Alright we must be on to something. You know the drill (yes I sometimes make them work for it). As they sometimes say "third times a charm" and there it was. In a song...NEVER ALONE. BINGO! We have a winner Johnny and that is how the title was finalized.

It has to make sense to you—like the Campbell Soup Can and scent of Chicken Noodle Soup in the previous chapter. Just remember to thank your Angels as they do due diligence. They want to be appreciated and loved too, just like you.

Chapter 4
SCENT OF AN ANGEL

Angels descending, bring from above, Echoes of mercy,
whispers of love.~Fanny J. Crosby

Have you ever noticed an aroma of sorts that reminds you immediately of someone you knew or a familiar odor that makes you stop and think "why is that so familiar?" The scents of a cigarette or cigars, chicken noodle soup, Ben-Gay, perfume, bacon and eggs, paint. It could be anything that has significant meaning to you and brings you back to a moment with a loved one passed. Say hello to who you think may be visiting and you'll be surprised. For me, usually as soon as I identify them they leave. They just stopped in to say "Hi" and want you to know they're with you. Sometimes it's a little bit more.

Bacon & Eggs

I remember waking one morning to the aroma of freshly made bacon and eggs, assuming Todd, my husband, was making his breakfast as he got ready for work.

Eventually he made it back to the bedroom where I was still lying in bed for that last few moments of relaxation before starting to get the kids ready for school. "Did you make extra bacon for the kids?" I asked. His response was something along the lines of what are you talking about? Apparently he did not make bacon and eggs. I was really looking forward to having some bacon after smelling it for the past 30 minutes.

On with the morning--got the kids off to school, got my self ready for work, in the car I go and now I smell bacon and eggs again? What in the world I'm thinking to myself, shrugged it off and kept driving. I arrive at work, got settled in, sit at my desk and guess what? Yup, I smell bacon and eggs. "Does anybody else smell bacon and eggs?"I asked all of my co-workers.

The aroma had been following me ever since this morning and I didn't understand it. A few of my co-workers smelled it too. Wow this is pretty powerful. And then it hit me-- Jodge – that's what we would call my grandfather from my dad's side of the family.

I remembered a camping trip he took with us when I was younger and he would get up early in the morning and cook up some good ole' fashion home style bacon and eggs. I was sleeping in the camper when the smell awakened me. Smelling it again brought me back to that special moment in time when he was with us on a trip to Lake Wallenpaupack and I related that smell to that moment.

I said "Hello Jodge, How ya doing? It's nice to have you around. I love and miss you." and then the scent that had followed me all morning long quietly disappeared.

Chicken Noodle Soup

Do you recall the story I told when I was having a reading by TLC Star Rosie on "Angels Among Us"? My Mom came through with the can of Cambells chicken noodle soup to validate that when I smelled her homemade chicken noodle soup it was her popping in to say "Hi!"

Refer back to Chapter 2 'Inspiration from Heaven' to reread the story.

Ben-Gay

Todd's grandmother lived to be 93! Which also meant many aches and pains as well as arthritis. Using Ben-Gay muscle rub was a constant in her later years. When we would visit her in her apartment complex, the second you opened the door, the fumes between the heat being so high and the Ben-Gay were enough to burn your lungs. Inevitably this is a scent that is easily recognizable for anyone in our family. Many of us have smelled this all too familiar fragrance many times--- knowing it is her.

Cigarettes & A Hug

I had received many visits from mother but not from my father and I really longed to hear from him. I had a reading once where he told me I didn't need him anymore, I was strong enough with out him. But he's my daddy and every little girl always needs her daddy.

He was a big smoker. In fact, he died from lung cancer, probably as a result from his smoking amongst other things. He did quit eventually and many years went smoke free before he was diagnosed with that dreadful disease.

One day when I was working in my home office, the scent of a freshly lit cigarette appeared and I immediately took notice. I start sniffing around the room to make sure nothing was on fire. The odor begins to get stronger and I ask "Dad, is that you?" I proceed to have a little conversation with him (well really I'm talking to my self because nobody is talking back per say) when I felt compelled to sit on the floor.

As I do so I grabbed my knees and hold myself into a ball like position and just burst into tears, as the flood gates open and I can't stop crying. No words were spoken when I suddenly felt this **amazing warmth surround me** as if I were receiving a hug.

I remember saying "Thanks dad I really needed that" and the sensation was gone and the tears stopped flowing as quickly as they started. I got up and went on with my day as if nothing had happened. That was the first time I had ever experienced such a quick and sudden overwhelming feeling - I know what I felt and it was one of my dad's great big bear hugs that I had been longing for for years.

Sometimes these experiences last for a while and in other moments it's just a split second. The first time the aroma appears, you'll never forget it and it will be easier to recognize the next time they visit.

The Scent of a Cigar

Growing up my husband's Grandfather smoked cigars. Like most children he thought his Grandpa was the best! He remembers his big hands and the strength of his stature and the smell of those cigars. He even remembers the brand "White Owl."

Every brand had it's own flavor and distinct fragrance and when he smells this scent he knows – it's grandpa. Todd can get a hint of this scent where ever he goes, be it work, a walk in the park, the grocery store. It's only there for a second, it doesn't linger - it's here and it's gone but he knows it's him just saying "hey I'm here – I'm with you."

Old Spice that's Nice– as told by Ann S.

A couple of days before my Mother had passed I would smell cigarette smoke and Old Spice. Those two together. I walked into the house and the smell of cigarette smoke was so intense I was like "where is that coming from?" I was walking around the house smelling and smelling and as I walked by Morgan's room I asked her "Honey are you smoking? Like seriously it's OK but are you smoking?" She responded "NO I do not smoke." The smoke was so heavy in her room but she didn't smell it. I told her grandpa is here.

She was only 9 months old when he died so she really didn't have a chance to get to know him. She doesn't remember him at all. He worshiped her and he always wanted to be with her.

The scent was so very strong and coming from the room where she was packing to go to college. I was rest assured that she was going to be OK.

Never Alone – Michelle Irene

Chapter 5
THE POWER OF MONEY

When angels visit us,
we do not hear the rustle of wings, nor feel the feathery touch of the breast of a
dove; but we know their presence by the love they create in our hearts.
Mary Baker Eddy

Do you find pennies or other coins in odd places? If you see a coin you notice it right? You may even pick it up, especially if it's heads side up.

This is a great way for your Angels to get your attention, especially if you're not noticing other signs they may be giving you. Hence the term "pennies from heaven." Coins are an item that are quickly and easily recognizable. They are shiny and capture your attention because of the familiarity.

My Dad was a big collector of dimes, and so when I find dimes where they don't belong, I know it's just him saying "hello."

They don't have to be just coins. Your Angels may place a small object that may have some sort of special meaning to you (marbles, feathers, flowers, playing cards) in random places, where they do not normally belong just to get your attention. They like to play and have fun too. You just have to notice and acknowledge, and it will probably continue to happen more often.

They may also be trying to send you a message. What were you doing, thinking or working on when you found your object? Does it relate to your relationship with someone special, a memory? What are your surroundings and how is this significant to you or to them?

It could be words of encouragement to move forward or to trust your intuition. Of course it's up to you to decipher the true meaning as you move forward. If you're not sure, just ask. They will answer again in the future.

At a Drop of a Dime

As a young child our family enjoyed camping. One of the best times of the day was at dusk when the sun was settling in for the night. We would start the campfire and join around in our folding chairs. Many times we would talk, sing songs, and tell stories. One story that really remained with me was one my dad would tell us over and over again about his grandfather.

My great grandfather enjoyed his much needed mug of beer after a long hard day's work in the coal mines of Pennsylvania. The name of the bar at the time was "Gin Mills" but later changed to Sokolowski's. For some unknown reason my great grandmother refused to give him his dime one day which of course did not make him very happy. Frustrated and exhausted he looked up to the heavens and said "I really could use my beer!"

As soon as he spoke he heard a coin drop sound 'ping' on the kitchen table. He got up from his chair and walked to the table and there it was. A dime!!!! Without hesitation he picked up the dime, gave it a kiss while showing it to the ceiling and said "I don't know who you are, but thank you." and went to the tavern to get his beer.

After recollecting this story it reminded me that my dad used to collect dimes. He would save them from his change when he would purchase lunch at work. At that time cigars used to come in a tin cylinder with a screw top and they were perfect for putting the dimes in. Once they were filled he would bring them home and place them in his sock drawer for a rainy day. I wonder if this was the reason my Dad collected dimes.

So the tradition of finding the dimes in odd places seems to carry on:

One day, when I was really having a rough time missing my parents, I felt the need to clean out my purse. Why I chose to clean out my purse I do not know. As usual I would take things out, place them on the counter to organize. Then clean out the pockets to make sure all the loose change, pens and garbage is out. One more glance around to make sure everything is out before that one last shake upside down to get rid of crumbs or dirt that may have accumulated and made there way to the bottom. As I was shaking it out the crumbs fell, as well as one little ole' dime.

I smiled, picked it up, gave it a little kiss while raising it to sky and said "Thanks dad, I love you too."

But wait, there's more...

While writing this book I have also been in the process of opening up a new store front with a unique gift shop filled with many locally made items. The store was once the bookstore that my mother managed for over 25 years, so it was exciting and a bit uncanny in a way the first few times I went in there.

I remember all the times I would walk in there and go straight to the back where the office was located and peak my head around the corner of the door to see my mother so diligently working. She would look up and smile her sweet smile and say hello.

The first time I went to look at the space with the realtor (after it had been vacant for a good length of time) I did the same thing....I walked right to the office area and peaked around the corner – the desk was still there. I had to take a moment to let it all soak in hoping I could feel her presence with me at this moment.

I negotiated a deal with the landlord because I felt it was the space I needed to be in. Starting on the renovations, the first thing we did was to remove the temporary wall that was the office to open up the store space. As we finally got to the metal studs and removed the bottom piece, guess what we found? Yup you guessed-it a dime. I shouted in excitement "I can't believe it!"

A few days later I was moving some shelving units in the back room and yes siree, I found another dime!

The clincher was moving a large counter unit to the back room and out fell a little yellow note card. Yellow was the color my mother despised the most, and on the card was her handwriting with a number in the top right hand corner - #10.

Remember earlier I said something about how I like things in sets of three? That confirmed it for me. Mom and dad were with me supporting me through all my efforts with this endeavor and I couldn't be more excited.

Just to show you, how when you finally realize some of the signs they leave behind and begin to notice, they really enjoy playing along with you and will show you signs more often.

We have a wonderful mother and daughter team who come to clean our house once a month and I was telling them the stories of the dimes. And the mother was smiling as I was telling the story. She confirmed that she will find dimes and pennies in odd places throughout the house when she is dusting. This made me smile and reassured me that my dad is really with me.

One evening on our daily walk with the dog, my husband and I were chatting away when I looked down and right in from of me was a circular object. I bent down to pick it up and wasn't quite sure if it was a dime or not. It had been run over and worn down by the rocks and salt from the winter. It looked like a dime so I put it in my pocket. When we got home I took a photo of it with my cell phone so I could enlarge it to examine. Sure enough it was a dime, almost clearly warn down except for the wording God Trust. Something my dad would often say "Trust in God."

I have a friend who likes to randomly drop pennies for others to find. She sends a tiding of love along with it in hopes that whoever finds it and picks it up will feel the love radiate in their life. By sending out the frequency vibrations through the universe, I'm sure the Angels are making certain that the right people are finding the coins left behind. Now that's an earth angel spreading love and joy to others.

Chapter 6
BIRDS OF A FEATHER

All God's angels come to us disguised. ~James Russell Lowell

Angels are associated with other flying creatures here on this earth most likely because of their ability to fly. Birds and other winged friends are sometimes sent for reassurance, peace, and comfort or sending a message of love.

You may see them in your waking hours or they may come to you in your dreams. Who knows, maybe when they are chirping and singing in harmony they are actually sending you a message?

The Messenger

I will never forget it. It was just a few days after my birthday and I wasn't feeling well. I had decided to lie down and take a nap. I cuddled up with my little buddy who was just a puppy at the time, a Bichon named Jeter, and we both fell fast asleep.

Now in a dream state I felt like I was outside in the middle of a place similar to the Grand Canyon. It was beautiful, quiet and extremely peaceful. No one was around, it was just me and the great outdoors.

I spotted something moving out of the corner of my eye and there it was. The most beautiful Bald Eagle I had ever seen.

Standing tall, head up and swoosh, it takes off from it's perch. It flies through the opened canyon space and away it went soaring high into the sky gliding forward.

I awoke from my sleep with a startle and a revelation – Otta (that's what we called my grandfather on my mother's side) had just passed away. Within 30 seconds the phone rang and it was my mother to let me know that Otta had just passed away.

Not only can the birds give you a message in your dream they can also deliver messages when you are awake. This is one of my favorite angel bird stories I've ever come across.

My Little Birdie – Told by Ann S.

When my Mom was sick with dementia we would sit and talk on a daily basis. One day we had a conversation about when we die, what happens? I explained what happens and her response was "how do we know that?" I told her " you taught me that Mom" and that lead into our pact saying whoever dies first the other has to come back somehow and let us know they are OK.

She then asked me, "well is that allowed?" and I responded "I don't know, we will have to find out." We had this conversation a lot.

On the day she passed I had a class to teach (Ann is a very predominate dance teacher in the area). It was the first day of classes for the summer so I had to go. Everybody who was at the house for condolences had already left for the day when I hear some racket in the kitchen. So I go into the kitchen and there is a bird flying around. I opened all the windows because I have to get rid of the bird and get to my class. The bird landed on a set of steps. I walked over to look at it and in a moment I had a sense that this was something special.

The bird went up the stairs and I went up a different set of stairs when I find the bird again sitting right on top of the step. I knelt down to get right in it's face, cupped my hands, and the bird went right in my hands.

It was just a very little brown wren, nothing special. At that moment I knew I was holding a piece of Heaven. I knew this was my Mom coming back to let me know.

I put the bird down and went to pick it up again. Now in my hands, I opened the sliding glass door put it out on the deck and immediately I wanted to share this with someone, I didn't want it to just be me.

So I prayed "Jesus please let me share this with somebody" Right away I hear the car door, I hear laughter, it's my daughter Morgan and her good friend. I yelled to her to quickly come up the stairs! The bird never even moved when I yelled and she comes running up the stairs and is standing next to me.

I'm looking at the bird and tell her this is grandma. I put her down and told her I had to leave to teach my class. When I was done with the class I went back to my house, threw my things down and looked at my husband Jim and he said "I know, Morgan is up stairs." I ran up the stairs and found Morgan.

Morgan and my mom were best buddies and she was leaving the next day for college. Morgan proceeded to tell me that she held grandma for a while and her friend Morgan held grandma. They put her down and said "if you are a hurt bird we will figure it out but if this is you grandma, it's OK you can go."

The bird turned – took a couple of steps to face her and flew away.

Such an incredible experience to read about, let alone to actually be the ones to witness such a beautiful piece of heaven. The visits do not end here:

God is Real - told by Ann S.

I called my brothers immediately after the "bird Mom" visitation. My brothers are awesome people but they think I'm a little crazy. They listened to the story with the bird and were very supportive except for my one brother – he was very angry and upset with me because he wanted a sign.

"What makes you so special?" he said to me.

A couple of days later I read "when a beautiful miracle happens for you, do not brag; do not talk about it. It makes it sound like you are more special than anyone else." That hurt. I felt so horrible because I never thought about it that way. I thought things happen so you share them.

After my mom's funeral I had some classes to teach. I am walking one of my teacher's baby in the parking lot when there was a plane that flew overhead. Whenever I see a plane with the sun hitting it just right I think of my dad. I'm talking to the baby now "OK there's grandpa, wouldn't it be so cool if we saw grandma again?" Out of the shadows walks this little bird coming right towards me. I bent down to pick it up and told the baby, because I figured I could talk to him about it. When I put down the bird I hear "Ann, were you just holding a bird?" I look and it's my neighbor and I said "YES" so I picked it up again and I'm holding it, I tell him the whole story.

His wife had just passed from ovarian cancer and we were having the conversation about is this God? Yes it is. It starts to rain and I say goodbye to Jack. I go into the studio with the baby and I'm giving him a bottle. I'm not going to say a word to anybody because I'm keeping it quiet but I want to scream it to everybody!

Then I hear my good friend Meg say "Ann, look" The bird had made it's way from the parking lot out into the foyer of the studio. Meg says "look, there's a bird right there." She had heard the first story. I walked over to pick up the bird. It's the little scruffy black and white bird, he looked like he was all beat up. Now I'm holding the bird.

My mother used to sit behind the desk at the studio and collect the money. If you owed any money my mother would let you know. Then it came over me, that was my mom simply saying "I'm here at the studio to let everyone know it's not about the money, the money means nothing, and I need to share this with everyone."

I now have my back turned to everybody and I'm hearing "put the bird down," "bird's have germs." I turn around with the bird and now I'm overcome and I just said "You know my mom just passed away and I believe this is her to let us know, it's not the money, God is real. This is all real. This is what's important."

My teachers came out and heard the story, feeling as if I had fabricated the story to fill my heart. I decide it's time to release the bird so I go outside to free it.

At the same time my mother's really dear friend , Judy, was on her way to pick up her granddaughter from dance class. The bird flies away and lands on a mini van. I look at Judy and she says, "You really think that's your mother?" I respond "There is no doubt in my mind. That is my mom and everything is good!"

Judy walks over to the van puts her arm up, the bird jumps in her hand, runs down her arm, looks like it gives her a little peck and flies away.

How amazing is that? Not only did this happen once but it happened twice within days of each other. I was so amazed by Ann's story and told her as such, then she proceeded to tell me it happened a third time!!!

Life Goes On – Told By Ann S.

This was the day I took my daughter to school. Everything was great, everything was great, I kept telling myself because I really was dreading it. My brother had just been diagnosed with cancer, my mother had just passed away, my daughter is going away to school, and it's an empty house. I was a mess. The next morning....now I'm not one to really feel depressed but I literally couldn't move, I was so devastated because I didn't know what to do with myself. I heard the racket again, I said to myself "Are you kidding me?" I wanted it to be my mom. I just couldn't put my faith in it at that moment. I've got to do something so I grabbed the garbage bag and I figured I would clean out all the garbage in the house, go outside, get in my car and go. Just drive. I didn't know where.

As I' took the garbage up the stairs, there was a bird sitting there, on the window sill. There are no doors open because I had not been outside, there are no windows open because I didn't have the strength to open them. I looked at that bird and I sat there and cried for the longest time.

I picked up the bird, went outside and let it go. I got in my car and drove. I went to the Parkway and just drove up and down just so I could be doing something.

That was the last time I saw the bird. I feel it was my Mom letting me know "life goes on, get over it."

What a gift! Isn't it amazing how God can send you a spiritual message through a bird? This is also a validation that it is ok to share these stories...it's more than OK. Ann feels that her Mother's dementia in a way was a gift. Because she never wanted to have that talk with anybody. The talk about death and her illness allowed her to do just that – over and over.

 People need to know that these visits are real and they can happen to you if you just listen and pay attention to the clues that are being sent to you by your Angels.

Chapter 7
I'M A DREAMER

*Millions of spiritual creatures walk the earth
Unseen, both when we wake and when we sleep.
~John Milton, Paradise Lost*

Have you ever received a message or a visit from a loved one in your dreams and felt it was so real? Chances are this really was a visit from your loved one. It is a non threatening way for them to visit you. Visiting in your dream takes much less energy and they know that when you are in your dream state, they have your attention! You are in an altered state when you are sleeping and your levels of understanding are greater, this is why it works well as a way of contacting you.

Before you go to sleep at night, ask for them to visit you. Keep a journal next to your bed so you can write things down as soon as you wake up. Often times when we wake in the middle of the night we think we'll remember our dreams in the morning and we usually forget before our feet hit the ground. Then it's gone and you can't evaluate whether is was a dream or a visitation.

However, in my experiences, I have found that if it was a true visit with a sound message, it feels so real, so vivid, unlike a regular dream that you will probably remember it in complete detail for the rest of your life.

I Love You

My dad had this thing about 'I Love You' being the last words he would ever say to you. He wouldn't say good bye on the telephone he would say "I Love You" and then hang up. He wouldn't say good bye as you were walking out the door, he would say "I Love You." It used to drive me crazy because I didn't understand why he wouldn't say good bye, like he was ignoring me.

Until one day I finally asked him why he never says good bye. His response was simple "because if anything happens to one of us after that last visit 'I Love You' would be my last words to you." Ahhhh I get it now, I understand and I love it.

When we were in the hospital and dad's time was diminishing, as a family we were surrounding him with love and stories trying to keep him as comfortable and happy as could be in this difficult time. We wanted him to know how much he was loved.

My oldest brother and I always bickered (still do) and that night was no different except it was all in good fun. My mom turns to my dad and says, " Joseph what do think about that, the kids are still arguing?" After he mustered up the strength to speak his response and sounding a bit like a sheep he says "baaaaa dddd"-- we all chuckled because he was joking around with us knowing we were just kidding too.

He wasn't talking much that day and I remember thinking OMG(oh my gosh for you non techy people out there) what if those were his last words to me – BAD – really? No, it couldn't be after all these years of attempts to make sure "I Love You" were his last words, this is how it's going to be?

Dad never spoke another word that evening and the following morning is when he went off to meet Jesus and the rest of his family who had since gone.

I was, of course, because he had passed away but also because of what his last words were to me. At moments I would laugh because it was kind of cute, and then, at other moments, it really bothered me. I tried to make light of it knowing he didn't really think I was bad and that he loved me with all his heart. I couldn't get past it.

"C'mon dad give me a sign," I would often say to myself.

A few months had passed and it was early in the morning when my husband woke from a good night's rest that I would finally get the response I was waiting for.

Todd looks at me with such love in his eyes and tells me he had a visit from dad last night. Excited, and a bit perturbed he didn't visit me, I responded in a fun loving way "Oh, you're so lucky, what happened".

He proceeded with the story about how real it felt and how short the visit was. We were in a restaurant – just the three of us. We were sitting in a booth and there was one light shining down on our table – lighting it up with love. There was no one else in the picture or anything else around our booth, it was complete darkness. Just the three of us in a booth with the light of love. Dad and Todd were sitting together on one side and I was sitting on the other side so they were both looking at me. He reaches across the table to grab my hands and looks deep into my soul through my eyes. Then he says it, "I Love You" with the most divine feeling of honesty, warmth, love and that was it. He was gone, the dream was over.

He came through to Todd to give me the three words I so longed to hear to be the last words that he would ever speak to me "I Love You"

Why he came to Todd instead of me I will never know. Maybe he felt I wasn't ready to receive this message direct --he always had this way of trying to protect me. It didn't make a difference to me how the message came through, it just did.

Sometimes when you're loved ones pass they are able to reach you immediately and leave you with a message just to let you know it will be OK or they will be OK. Letting us know that there is more after we go and that we are never alone.

World War II sweethearts, Robyn's mom and dad were in love from the very beginning and that love carried over...

Visitation with a Good-bye Gift as told by Robyn

The night that he passed, she saw my dad, her husband. Shirley, Robyn's mom recalled the experience "He came to me and said "Shirley I can't stay, but don't cry." He was riding in a Bronco with two other guys on their way home from a fishing trip in Canada when they drove off a cliff and landed on the railroad tracks. When the men in the car came back to consciousness they tried to wake my dad. They didn't get any movement and they didn't dare move him.
Trains seldom rode on these tracks so they felt OK leaving him behind. They climbed the embankment to get help. While

in search of assistance, a train came and hit the Bronco. The conductor was a Frenchman and he said that he (Robyn's dad) was still alive. He was calling out his wife's name, as the conductor repeated it while telling the story in his French accent sounding like "Shiree Shiree."

Sometimes in your dreams your angels can teach you or help you to solve a problem. Here is an instance when my son Derek was taught a special lesson from his grandfather.

Filet A Fish

My parents spent a lot of time with my children as they were growing up. They built some great relationships and wonderful memories that they carry with them forever.

One of my dad's most favorite past times with Derek was to go fishing. He took my brother's and I fishing many times when we were kids as well. It wasn't about fishing, it was about the time spent together. Through the years Derek has continued to be an avid fisherman. It was only fitting when my dad passed that my mom gave Derek some of dad's fishing equipment including his filet knife. He never got a chance to show Derek how to use it but Derek cherished it none the less.

As time went by my dad decided to pay Derek a visit during a dream. He told him how sorry he was that he never had a chance to show him how to use the knife.

I want to teach you. He went through each step from the head to the tail and all the other steps in between like trimming off the scales to slicing it in half and removal of the bones to prepare for cooking. Derek was with him by his side the entire dream as Dad talked him through each step with such precision and detail. He knew it was a visit from his Grampa Joe and now he knew exactly how to prepare a filet a fish.

This dream was so real and vivid that even though years have passed, he hasn't forgotten how to filet a fish.

I remember having situations where I couldn't quite figure out a new design and I would struggle for hours or days and sometimes just put it on a shelf in hopes that somewhere down the line I will figure it out. There have been times where the idea or a solution would come to me in a dream and they usually worked. I don't remember a special angel showing me but I do remember thanking the good Lord for helping me out. Angels are not just there for big large miracles they are there to guide you and help you even with the smallest situations or to get you through a trying time. Just like this special birthday gift in the next story.

11-27 as told by Joanne

I lost my 16 year old in 1989. In 2003, one of his very best friends, who I still keep in touch with (I'm the Godmother to one of his children), had contacted me on Christmas Day that year.

He said, "I had a dream last night about Steve and I haven't dreamed about him all these years." He proceeded to tell me how he said he was doing well and to tell my mom I miss her and I will contact her on 11-27. He told me he didn't know if it was morning or night, if it was a date. It was clear as could be and then he just faded away.

He wasn't sure if he should tell me this message, but his wife Cindy said, "Oh yes, she would want to know this." He just didn't want to upset me, after all it is Christmas.

Now every time I see 11-27 I'm looking at the clock morning and night but to no avail. No message. No contact. It didn't happen so I moved on thinking it may never occur, however, I did keep it in the back of my mind.

In February, on what would have been Steven's 30th birthday, my family and I decided to go out for pizza. A very low key evening. We came home and they all went to bed. I'm just relaxing on the couch by myself.

At this time I was home schooling my son Kevin who was in middle school. I had this stop watch which he loved to use to time things like his multiplication tables and it would sit on the kitchen table. The family room and kitchen are like one big room, they are open to each other. I'm on the sofa just looking at Steven's picture thinking about him and all of a sudden the alarm on the stop watch just starts to go off.

It had never done this before. I ran to the table and just as I'm picking it up, it stops! I look at the time on the stop watch and it's 11:27.

What are the chances that this would have happened on his birthday with those exact numbers on the clock!

Birthday messages seem to be a popular time for Angels of our loved ones to stop in for a moment or even a message.

My son Derek had a dream on his last birthday that he and his wife to be at the time, were going to a Maroon 5 concert. Why Maroon 5 he does not know, but that really has no relevance to the story.

The concert was in an outdoor stadium and when they finally were about to find their seats, there was someone sitting in one of them.

Derek proceeds to tell the gentleman, "Excuse me sir, but these happen to be our seats." When the man turned around it was Grandpa Joe!

"Oh I know Derek, we just want to wish you a Happy Birthday." Derek asked them to stay and then my Dad tells him that they have the best seats in the house as he points up to the sky and will be watching up there.

They really do show up in so many different ways, shapes and forms. If you have a certain problem that is difficult to solve just ask before you go to sleep at night.

If you want a visit from a loved one, just ask. It may not happen right away.

Remember to keep that paper and pen next to your bed to write your dreams down as soon as you wake up. The solution may not always be obvious but it's probably there. You may have to siphon through and read between the lines.

Be patient. It will come.

Chapter 8
DO YOU HEAR WHAT I HEAR

Make yourself familiar with the angels, and behold them frequently in spirit; for, without being seen, they are present with you. ~St Francis of Sales

Blinking lights, ceiling fans, stopping watches, draining batteries from tech devices, turning off or on a television are all signs that spirit is around. When you ask for a sign does a special song come on the radio? Do you randomly start singing a song and don't know why that just indiscriminately popped in your head?

In this chapter you will see some amazing examples of how the Angels can visit through technical devices.

Jiggle The Handle

Growing up our toilet would run quite often after you were done flushing it. You know that sound of running water because the tank is trying to fill up, but because the plunger thingy (very professional word) isn't covering the hole properly it can't do the job it's supposed to do. It was annoying to say the least.

Anyways, as a child you would do your bathroom thing, flush, wash, and out you go. Being that the bathroom was directly down the hall from the living room, where we spent most of our time, you could hear it running. This annoyed my dad to no end. "Jiggle the Handle!" he would yell out to who

ever was near by, which made it even more annoying.
This ritual eventually became an on going joke in the family.
I can recall buying him a birthday card one year in regards to
"jiggle the handle' and it got good laughs.

So on the evening that my father passed, this event was of no
surprise to me. The family had all gathered at my home (not
the one I grew up in) where the toilet on the main floor never
ran. We were sitting around the dining room table sharing
memories and making plans for the funeral services when all
of a sudden (no body had even flushed it) the toilet started to
run. We all stopped what we were doing and it was silent. I
walked to the bathroom, jiggled the handle, looked upward
and said, "your funny Dad! Thanks."

Needless to say we all had a good laugh and the toilet has
never had to be "jiggled" again. It's nice to know you don't
lose your sense of humor even in Heaven.

Apparently my parent's sense of humor in the after-life is a
continuation because they were immediately throwing out signs
that they were with us and put on shows of many kinds. Here are
a few more:

I Don't Like That Picture

You know those picture boards that we all feel the need to
create when a loved one passes? You know, the one's that
make you cry more as you look through amazing memories
of their life?

During my dad's funeral service the photo board was on an
easel next to the casket.

There was this one picture that Dad just did not like. He didn't like it because he was bald from his treatments but I thought he was the cutest bald man ever and he had such a jolly smile on his face. I thought it was adorable, so of course I had it on the picture board.

Throughout the service this picture fell off more than once. I went to pick it up, stick it back on, but each time I rehung it, it would just fall off again. I finally decided to get the tape to give it some extra stickiness because this photo is going to stay on thc board!

While the priest was giving his sermon we are all sitting in the chairs facing the casket, and yes, this picture decides to fall off again even after I added more tape.

I chuckled to myself and realized this was dad putting on a little show and letting us know he really doesn't like this picture.

It was really of no surprise when my mother passed that she was quite capable of letting us all know she was still with us.

Where is that CD?

The night before my mother's viewing, my brother and I offered her two sisters to stay at my parents house so they wouldn't have to pay for a hotel. It was nice to have someone there, it just felt comforting. I think my mom agreed.

They stayed up late talking and sharing stories while sitting in the living room. On the end table was a CD player and some

CD's that mom enjoyed listening to on her last days at home. So my aunt's started shuffling through the titles and found an album they wanted to listen to. They opened the case and of course it was empty. They opened the cd player and it wasn't in the player. They looked around the house for a short time but could not find the cd.

They finally decided to call it a night and went to bed. One aunt went to sleep in my parent's room and the other went to sleep in the guest room. Around 3:00 in the morning the cd player next to my mom's bed turned on playing the album they had been in search of earlier. Not only did it turn on and play but it was so loud it woke up my other aunt in the next room!

Needless to say they spent the rest of the night in the living and didn't go back to sleep.

Angels love to play with music. I remember a moment when I was deciding on the name for this book and asked for a message of reassurance when a song came on the radio and within a few moments I heard the words Never Alone in the verse. Sometimes they can send a message through a song just like the next story:

Music with a Message – as told by Robyn B.

When my daughter was born I named her after my father. She was the first baby in the family with red hair and blue eyes...just like him. His name was Lawrence and I named her Lawreen, Lawrence with no C. That same year the song "In The Living Years" by Mike and The Mechanics came out. That was a song I listened to often. The song came out after we named our daughter. The first time I ever heard that song it connected me to that whole scenario of my daughter, my father, and myself.

That was his way of telling me,I know about you and your daughter, my Granddaughter.

Loved ones can come through in so many ways and if you recognize and really listen you may even hear a message.

The Red Hat

One evening, my family, including Taylor's boyfriend Kurtis, were having dinner while I was on my way out the door for a meeting. "Mom the ceiling fan just randomly turned on," Taylor says as I'm leaving the house to attend a meeting. Since I was in a rush I didn't think much of it and just shrugged it off. I mean every time there is an electrical surge you can't just automatically assume it's a visit from a loved one.

A few days later we all were having dinner again, including me, and the ceiling fan went off again. I immediately felt as if this is Alan, Kurtis' dad. (Trust the first thing that comes to mind).

Kurtis had the misfortune of losing his father at a young age. Not really being a believer in the after-life (until he came into our family), he had been hoping for some sort of sign that his Dad was OK and was with him.

As the thought enters my mind that this is Kurtis' dad, I hear a voice say, "ask him about the hat, the red hat,"
I didn't immediately ask him and kept this to myself for

months. Knowing that Kurtis was somewhat of a skeptic and not really too sure of my listening skills, I finally said something to Taylor about my message and asked her about the red hat. Taylor then told me that their favorite baseball team was the Cincinnati Reds. She proceeded to tell me that at one of the games they attended together, his father bought him a new Cincinnati Reds hat.

Confirming that indeed this was a visit from his dad, and also confirmation of one of the first messages I clearly remember hearing, and was able to deliver ~ delayed but delivered.

The ceiling fan has not turned on by itself since this last happening and it's been almost a year!

My grandfather decided when he passed that he wanted to let his wife know. Read on.

Stopped Watch

At the time of my grandfather's passing he was in a nursing home. At the exact time of his death his wristwatch stopped. The watch was back at his residence, not at the nursing home. Not only that, but his cane was standing in the corner of his apartment, when it fell to the ground, alerting my grandmother to his passing.

To be able to receive a message you have to learn how to listen – really listen. If words pop into your mind trust them. Don't think, just trust and you most likely will be able to receive. We all have the capabilities to receive.

Chapter 9
LIGHT UP MY LIFE

Never Travel faster than your guardian angel can fly – Mother Teresa

I have a tendency to see angels as you would see a star in the sky. It's like a little star that twinkles at night only it's in the room sometimes right on someone's shoulder or just hanging out in the corner. Just as quick as it appears it disappears and sometimes it may linger for hours! When it hangs around in the room is one of my favorite moments because I feel as if they are watching over my family while we are all together in one place. They may appear in moments of need for comfort, if you feel alone, or even if you just need some reassurance.

Seeing these forms of light, glowing orbs, flashes, etc...is reassurance of an angel in your presence. Sometimes the light can be as great as filling a whole room when it's completely dark. If you see these lights, you are experiencing the energy of the Angel/Spirit crossing the room, the White Light. Remember we are all energy, just in different forms. Take the time to reflect when you do see these forms of light and thank them for the moment.

An orb is another form of light that can be seen. Usually it is an unexpected round shaped light that shows up in a photograph. Sometimes you may see a trail which indicates it's movement. They are usually transparent and extremely hard to identify.

Scientists have attempted to identify these light beings but they have remained unexplained. In saying that, orb's are a tricky thing to identify because of their unproven mystic. They can be dust, bugs, moths, reflections, etc....so you have to rule out the possibilities before you can claim it as an orb, and even then, it's your claim and not factual.

Size is another factor in identifying these light forms (spots made from bugs and moths tend to be very small). If there are many other orb like visuals in the picture it usually represents dust from movement before the picture was captured. It's transparency and light surrounding it are another key factor. Most of the time, when an orb appears in a picture, it's just plain ole' instinct that pops into your mind. A knowing.

Angel On My Shoulder as told by Diane S.

When I was pregnant, knowing that I was going to lose the baby, there was a picture of me taken and in the picture there is an orb an Angel in my hand. I am not holding anything! The picture was taken on the 8th and we lost Rosemary on the 13th.

 *Check out the pictures of Diane with the same orb, minutes apart in two different pictures. If she didn't have the two photos, I would have chalked it up to a reflection of something in her hand, and then she showed me the orb sitting on her shoulder.

I was convinced. You can see the flash reflection in the mirror up above in both shots and it really has no bearing on the light resting on her shoulder or in her hand.

Diane with her special Angel Orb. I've never seen one like this before. At first glance I thought it was a reflection from something she was holding, then she showed me the other picture and the Angel is sitting on her shoulder. Incredible.

I'm not going to try to prove or disprove the theories behind orb light forces. You believe or you don't, but sometimes it's just a feeling that it's something more.

Watching Over Her

It was my daughter,Taylor's, first semester at college, which is always an adjustment period for any person entering school at that level. She was a scholarship athlete for the school's Softball Program.

During a team bonding event, they had a team photo taken and the only thing I noticed besides the smile on her face was the biggest orb I had ever seen, right next to Taylor. It stuck right out! No other little orbs surrounding it. I knew in an instant it was my Mother,
Taylor's grandmother, protecting her.

A few weeks later, when Taylor went for a reading with a local medium, the first thing she asked Taylor "Did you know you did not walk in here alone today? Your Grandmother is with you. She says she is always by your side protecting you."

*The orb next to Taylor (on the next page) in a Team photograph shows another example of what an orb can look light.

Taylor with her College Softball Team and a large Spiritual
Orb (above) A close up view of the orb (below) Later we
found out through a medium reading that her Grandmother
was with her often during her Freshman Year.

Here's another inspiring story of an orb offering protection.

The Orb Light – as told by Robyn B.

About 14 years ago we bought this wonderful house built in 1910. The second I walked into the house, I knew it was happy place. I knew there was nothing to be concerned with. It was a house that felt comfortable and safe. There were nine children who were raised there and only one family before us had lived there. You could just feel the love in the home. I never worried about anything.

About two years before that, I was starting to see this kind of orb-like light in my house. I never really was too concerned because I gave it to God. I have all trust there. I would see the light in my bedroom in the middle of the night and it would be there when I would wake – I knew I was awake, I would reach for it and it would throw itself back like I wasn't suppose to touch it. It happened often.

After awhile I just sort of ignored it. I just accepted that it was going to be there. Then I found out I had cancer. It was a difficult time. We didn't know what stage,we didn't know a lot of things for a while. We found out it was in the early stages and I started radiation treatments.

After all the treatments were done and we knew I was going to be OK— the orb was gone. It never showed up in my room again.

Sometimes you know who they are and other times you don't. Embrace it, regardless, that they have made themselves known to you and are there for your protection.

Night Light of Support – as told by Diane S.

I took care of my grandmother when she was ill before she passed away. I don't know why but for some reason I really wanted this one night light that was hers. The light never really worked, but I always kept it plugged in. Every so often it would light up especially at times when I was really struggling in life.

Shortly after her death, I started dating my now husband, I told him, "Just so you know my Grandmother lives in the night light," so don't ever throw this away. He responded with a typical response, "You know there is probably a short in it somewhere and it's going to burn your house down." This had been going on for years, it would be turned off for months at a time and then be on for days.

When we moved to our house, of course the light came with us. It had not turned on for a very long time now and I thought to myself, I really should get rid of this in case it does burn the house down.

The night before our wedding I stopped by the house to get something and it lit up in the kitchen. It got to the point where my husband would say, "Grandma is here." It was just so comforting.

Throughout my life I have been on a quest for information about the after-life, angels, spirits, etc... Knowing that I have a sort of intuitiveness, but not really sure what it is or what it all means. So I read, and read, and read and view any information I can get my hands on to better understand it all.

Before a family vacation on the Jersey Shore one summer, I

visited the library (this was before Kindle and Amazon) to sign out some books for the trip. It was in these books that I discovered the twinkling light that I was seeing was real and it was what I thought it was. An angel passing through. One of my favorite reads was a book called *Second Sight* by Judith Orloff, MD. She is a psychiatrist/psychic. It is the first book that I remember reading that actually touched on my experiences and what it all meant.

Things finally started to make sense to me and it was a relief. In the book she talked about the white light and it's spiritual reference. This was the first time I had remembered hearing this term. What was this white light?

The White Light is a protective field that you can call upon at anytime. It can be used for healing, protection, blocking out negativity, and bringing all your energies into balance for a healthy happy life.

Take a moment, close your eyes if you have to, take a deep breath and simply ask your Angels to surround you with the white light. You can ask them to surround others in your life with whom you want to protect. You don't have to see a white light you just have to trust in your Angels to fulfill your request. After you have asked for the assistance always make sure you thank them for this action. They like to be appreciated like you and I.

A Ray of Sun

On this same trip to the Jersey Shore I remember reading about the white light for the first time. I practiced asking it for protection for myself and my family. I would think about it while on the beach as the ocean waves came in and came out. I would ask for it's guidance on helping me to see more then just the little twinkle stars. (This was before my visit from PJ in our bedroom in NY). I was ready to embrace what they had to offer.

Not really getting any answers back and thinking well I guess maybe it's all just hogwash, or I'm doing something wrong, I had decided one more time to ask my Angels for a sign before I went to sleep one night.

I remember waking up partially and covering my face with my pillow thinking maybe I had fallen asleep with the TV on. The entire room was full of light. When I completely opened my eyes and realized no TV or lamp was turned on and it was 3 o'clock in the morning (and it was pitch black outside) it dawned on me, this was my sign. The sign that the white light of protection is real.

It was unlike any light I had seen before, almost like the sunshine was in our room. The colors illuminated like no other and it was warm physically and spiritually. I was in amazement and knew that it was an answer to my prayer that night for a sign.

Soaking it all in, I kindly thanked my Angels/Spirit Guides or whoever sent the light to me for allowing me to have this experience.

It has been amazing to me while writing this book that once you share with people what you are doing, an abundance of stories come to surface. People are so willing to share and I am so grateful to be able to share them back with you.

You've probably experienced moments of light without realizing it. It could be a glimpse into someone's eyes, a twinkle in the sky, or an entire room illuminating. It may also just be a feeling of loving warmth (no, hot flashes do not count). You never know when it may appear, but if you are aware, pay attention or just ask -- you may get a response back and a glimpse into the after-life.

Chapter 10
EARTH ANGELS

"Do not forget to entertain strangers, for by so doing some people have entertained angels without knowing it" (Hebrews 13:2, NIV)

Sometimes you are placed in someone's life because your angels can use you as a vessel to help a special someone out in time of need. Other times, when you are in need, the tables may be reversed and you are sent an Angel to help you along the way.

One moment they are here and the next they are gone. Have you ever experienced this before? Someone helps you out and you go to thank them and they are nowhere in sight? How about the time when you are in the grocery store or walking down the street and someone walks by you that looks just like your mother or your grandfather and you hesitate just for moment a bit confused, a bit bewildered, because of the uncanny resemblance? This is a moment when you think, "was that really" and your immediate response should, "yes, yes it was." That is your loved one reminding you they are with you, and you are Never Alone.

You're Her Angel

Sometimes along the way even the Best Friendships part ways, for many reasons, some of them unknown. Two woman set apart by circumstances so small, had slowly started to find their way back to each other before the news had hit.

"I have cancer." Why after all this time when we find our way back to each other does this have to happen?

My response was, "Because you're her angel and she needs your love and support so God has brought her back to you."

Hugs through an Earth Angel told by Maureen R.

I'm running late and I have two stops left with my errands for the day. One is Project Concern (it's a donation center where you can drop off household items and clothing for the less fortunate) or drop off this Angel Ornament I had for my friend who was really missing her recently deceased mother.

Project Concern is closing in 15 minutes. I decide to stop at Project Concern and drop off the ornament later. It's damp and raining and I walk in and there are three women standing there and they all simulated the sounds of Santa "HO HO HO Santa" (mind you it's just a few days before Christmas). One of the women spoke up and asked if I needed any help and I replied, "No, stay in side where it's warm and dry. I have a couple of more trips."

 I went back to my car to get the second load and I'm thinking, "Where do I know that woman from?" I went back in and looked her right in the eye and I'm thinking – "you don't look the least bit familiar to me but why do I know you?"

 I go back to my car for the third trip, go back in to the shop, and all of a sudden her voice again and it just hits me. I looked at her and said, "you're Denise." With no words spoken Denise comes over to me and gives me a hug (and the flood gates of tears have now opened).

She was the nurse who had taken care of my mother when she was dying. I said to her, "Never will I forget your Angel voice." Here I am trying to comfort my friend, Michelle, who is going through a tough time missing her recently deceased mother. Michelle says to me, "I don't know how you did it, I miss my mom so much," and I realized at that point that my mother had been gone 14 years now just 10 days carlicr. So I said to Michelle, "14 years later and my angels are still talking to me."

Later that day I went home and told my friend, "I haven't cried for months. You just never know when to expect it" I later told my husband, Tim, and I've been like a water faucet all day long. I'm not sad, I'm just really really touched.

This was her Mother's way of coming through to give her a hug.

Earth Angels come in so many different shapes and forms. You never know when you may need one or when they will appear.

A Helping Hand -- by Sarah P.

I went to Brazil when my family adopted my second brother. In order to adopt, my parents had to go and spend a month there, so they flew me out so I could be there for their last week. I was on a different flight home, they were flying directly to NY from Rio. I had to go to another city for a layover and then onto NY. I was leaving first; so I'm in Rio and they walk me to the terminal and I am thinking, "OK cool, I'm good. No worries" But once I get into the terminal, I realize there is no English and the place is gigantic. I cannot figure out where I am going and no-one around speaks English. I feel like a panic attack is coming on, so I do the smartest thing I can think of to do, and that is to sit down on a bench and start to cry.

This Brazilian man approaches me and asks "Do you need some help?" He speaks perfect English and I responded "Yes I do." I showed him my ticket and said this is where I am going. He then told me he is on the same flight and transferring to the same flight as me, "I'll take you with me and onto the same flight to NY as well," he said.

We get on our first flight to South Paulo—now mind you South Paulo is one of the biggest airports in Brazil and I have to take a shuttle to the next terminal. I would have never been able to do this on my own. He stays with me.

We get on our next flight and he approaches my seat and lets me know there are many open seats in the back of the plane. "You can lay down and rest," he says, knowing that it is a 10 hour flight. We finally arrive in NY, exit the plane and I see my parents. I turn to introduce this kind gentleman to every one and he was gone. He vanished.

I wanted everyone to meet him because he saved my life that day, I would probably still be on a bench crying. He disappeared before I had a chance to thank him – he took care of me through the entire journey. As quick as he appeared—he disappeared.

When the moment is taking place you may not realize that it is an actual Earth Angel. We have a tendency to be so caught up in the moment especially when caring for a loved one. In the next story you'll understand this a little bit more.

A Nurse in Disguise as told by my Aunt Barbara

It was years later when it occurred to me the that the visitor to Uncle Jerry's hospital room in Orlando had to have been an angel.

A rather large black woman who identified herself as a "substitute nurse" came into the room one night, looked at Uncle Jerry's chart, and shook her head as if to say, "That's not good." He had been running a high fever for days, he was on a cooling blanket, and I was constantly running cold cloths all over his body.

The doctor's couldn't find out why he had the fever, so all we were doing was cooling him down as best we could. His neurologist said, "The brain doesn't like heat," and in my mind I thought, "especially when it is healing."

That was about ten days after the initial surgery on his brain and my feet had never left the floor beside his bed. I never left the room, and somehow it was alright for me to lie down on the window seat bed and I slept for four hours.

I woke up to water running in his shower and panicked thinking I shouldn't have left his bedside wondering if the nurse had dragged him out of bed. Well, she didn't, and the next day the fever was gone, and I never saw her again and the nurses on the floor had no idea who I was talking about when I asked.

Just one of the many miracles I witnessed that kept Uncle

Jerry with me and leading almost a normal life all those extra years.

Sometime in uncertain moments amazing things can happen that have no explanation whatsoever. These moments are pure and another way of knowing we really are Never Alone.

Chapter 11
SAVING GRACE

For he will order his angels to protect you wherever you go. Psalm 91:11

There are moments when you know that something amazing and unexplainable has just taken place. Instances like these have been reported often and usually they are hard to believe unless they have actually happened to you. Just like the story in Chapter 10 about the nurse coming in the middle of the night to save my uncle. It's unexplainable but it was real. It happened. Your Angels are there to protect you when it's not your time to go.

A Moment In Time

One morning I was on my way to my parents house when I decided to stop for a cup of coffee at a local store. I was sitting in the line for the drive-thru service and looking at the car in front of me. For some reason I was really focusing on the details of the car. The family stickers that were on the back you know the ones, - stick figures of Dad, Mom, Kids, Dog, etc.... and the college decals stuck in the windows. As I'm at the window of the drive- thru I took note that the car had turned right and it felt like it just sort of disappeared. I distinctly remember thinking where did this car go?

I get my coffee, and drive forward to take the turn out of the parking lot, slowly moving up to the traffic light to take a right hand turn back onto the main strip. The light is red so I urn on my blinker in preparation, look left, look right, look left and at the same time the light turns green.

While I was looking both ways to prepare for the turn I noticed the oddest thing. All of a sudden the air changed. I can't explain it, it was heavier, almost like a slow motion, but yet I was still moving at the regular speed.

"Where did all the traffic go?"I remember saying out loud to myself. It was the busiest time of day and yet traffic had randomly stopped? There were no people around. It was eery to say the least.

As the light turns green and I begin to make the right hand turn....time starts rolling again. I hear a loud crash behind me at the intersection. There was traffic again EVERYWHERE and people were moving again!

As I looked in my rear-view mirror to see what just happened. I realize there was an accident at the intersection where I just turned from and it was the car that was originally in front of me. Wait, where did it come from? I distinctly remember it turning and disappearing. The car had no way of possibly getting behind me in that short amount of time. I distinctly remember looking in my rear view mirror and seeing no other vehicles behind me.

I pull off into the grocery store parking lot across the street for two reasons 1. I wanted to make sure that everyone involved was OK. 2. To get my wits together because I am really confused about what just happened. It felt as if time had literally just stopped. It stopped to protect me from this accident.

Luckily there were others there to help out the people involved. I sat in the car, stunned by the occurrence that just for a moment, time had stopped for me to pass through a potentially dangerous situation as my angels protected me from harm.

Here is another memorable moment in time when for just a blink of any eye, and the blink of a twinkling light --- protection was apparent.

Flash of Light As told by Sarah D.

I was driving my daughter to a friend's house one weekend afternoon and we were heading down Chenango Street towards Hillcrest. As I drove straight by Nowlan Road, a car turned from Nowlan right in front of me.

I flinched, saw a flash of white light, and expected to hear the smashing of cars. But the next thing I knew I was still driving straight through. I have no idea how there was no collision between my car and the one that pulled out in front of me. My heart pounding, I asked my daughter if she saw what just happened.

She was typing a text and missed the whole thing. In my heart I knew that flash of white light was angelic intervention that prevented what could have been a very bad accident.

After getting over the initial fright from such a "close call," I felt gratitude for the Angels that kept us safe that day.

I don't know how they do it but I have heard so many stories of Angels pushing, pulling, lifting, holding back to protect others from harm. It truly is amazing. Here is a story that Ben recollects from his childhood.

A Little Bit Of Help – As told by Ben M.

Years ago, I was maybe six or seven yrs. old, my family would spend hot summer evenings down on the Willamette River, swimming and having a BBQ. All the grownups were in the water swimming and playing. My brother and I were close to shore but working our way to deeper water.

Suddenly I stepped in a hole and went under. I got a mouth full of water, came back up spitting, went down again and was able to come up to the surface once more.

I yelled for help, but no one heard me, and I could see them but no one around had noticed I was in trouble. I went under again, swallowed more water, and fought to get back to the surface.

All of a sudden I felt hands grab me from behind and lift me out of the water and toss me towards shore. I turned around and looked to see who did that! None of the grownups were even close to where it happened. They still hadn't noticed anything was wrong.

To this day I have always wondered as to the intervention there that saved my life. I have never forgotten that day and still do not understand it.

"For the angel of the Lord guards and rescues all who reverence Him." Psalm 34:7

Chapter 12
SIMPLE REMINDERS

You Are Never Alone
Some one is always with you watching over you ~ Michelle Irene

There are moments when you see things, someone or an event takes place that is beyond coincidence. Like I have stated earlier, I don't really think there are coincidences, I think it's all part of God's Plan, but in case you do, maybe this will help you rethink the possibility.

A Gift From Heaven

While working one day at my shop, an old acquaintance came in search of gifts for the Holiday's. The anniversary of her young daughter's death was soon approaching and it never gets any easier. It's a tough day none the less.

Lisa proceeds to tell me how her oldest daughter is expecting her first child making this Lisa's first grandchild. Her due date had come and gone and still no signs of labor. Although the anniversary date of Justine's death was still a couple of weeks away, I told Lisa, " I bet that's the day your grandchild is going to be born. She wants to make it a happy day for you."

Sure enough, a couple weeks later on the exact date a new life was brought into this world, into this particular families life, making an otherwise sad day into a new day of celebration.

With every story I have heard, every experience I have had, it never loses my amazement when all of these simple reminders take place right before your very eyes.

'Words' of Encouragement

I had just finished with my first Angel Meeting at a local coffee shop. I had the opportunity to sit and chat with a morning coffee group about any experiences they may have had with angels.

It was a wonderful, heartwarming experience to listen and share in everyone's stories. While I was sitting there listening intently, I quickly got distracted by something on the shelf . There was shelving around the cafe where items made by local artists were displayed and being sold. One of the items was a hanging shelf (for lack of a better description) made from old books and hooks. A very unique object in itself, but that's not what distracted me.

There were four books total for this shelving unit and only two words POPPED out at me in utter disbelief. *Just Folks* was the title of the book.

This was the user name for my dad's email account! What? I had never seen those words together before, EVER! I couldn't believe it. Thank goodness I was recording this session because I got lost in the moment and was hoping I didn't miss any important details of the group member sharing her angel story.

 Right there and then I knew that my dad was with me at this meeting and he was approving of the adventure I was about to embark on.

Not until I was documenting this story did I realize another connection. The name of the coffee shop was "Cup Of Joe." Joe is my dad's name.

1 Truck 2 Truck – as told by Debbie S.

When my family would go on a road trip with my grandmother in the car, we would play car games to help pass time. My grandmother, for some reason, had a love for red 18-wheelers. So we would count all the red 18-wheeler trucks we could see on the way to our destination. It's been three years since she passed, but recently on a trip to Uncle Mike's downstate, we decided to play the game that grandma loved so much.

One truck, two truck, three. They were everywhere! Wow I just counted five in a row! When it was finally time to exit, we realized there was another red truck behind us, and it passed by our car just as we exited – like it was protecting us.

All in all there were 41, YES 41, red trucks on the way to our destination. We have never had that many before on a road trip. So I decided to count on the trip back home. Eight. Eight red trucks were all that we saw.

I believe this was Grandma who had joined us on the road trip down just letting us know she was with us.

Shooting A Star – as told by Doug D.

After my daughter Kristina's funeral, I went outside on the deck and looked up to the night sky. It was filled with stars and I asked for a sign to let me know she was OK. At that moment a shooting start shot across the night sky!

Doug proceeded to tell me how these stories and others you hear are hard to explain, but your heart tells you to believe that there are angels out there. Then he told me another story about his other daughter and granddaughter showing us there are simple signs from above.

A Special Birthday Wish – as told by Doug D.

My daughter Larissa called me after her birthday. She told me that her daughter, Ellie, my granddaughter, whose middle name is Kristina, at the age of two had wished her mother a Happy Birthday. Larissa's husband, John, was out of town so he could not have told Ellie to wish mommy a Happy Birthday. I told her it was her sister from Heaven whispering in Ellie's ear to tell mommy Happy Birthday!

What a special moment to have. A special birthday wish from your sister. How else would little Ellie know?

It's a Funny -- As told by Sarah D.

My husband's grandfather, William Hazlett, passed away years before we met. His grandmother, Evelyn, was one of the sweetest, most loving grandmothers, and our family was blessed to have her in our lives for as long as we did. She passed away at the age of 98 on March 25, 2014.

The following Thanksgiving my husband's mother brought some of grandma's items to our house that she thought we might like to keep. One of these items was a coffee mug that had belonged to my husband's grandpa and that his grandma had packed away and saved.

It was a Peanuts mug and had an image of Snoopy with his dog bowl full of food outside in the snow. It was captioned with "I hate when it snows on my French toast." My husband chose to keep this mug.
The following Sunday after Thanksgiving day my husband and I were relaxing in the morning with the newspaper. He found the comics, which are his favorite part of the Sunday paper and he couldn't believe what he saw. The Peanuts cartoon printed in that day's paper was the same one pictured on the mug that had belonged to his grandpa and that his grandma had packed away for safe keeping.

It was obvious that even though they weren't with us physically that holiday season, they were making their spiritual presence known with the Snoopy synchronicity. It was a comfort to know they sent us this message and we're still with us.

A Christmas Story –by told by Debbie S.

Grandma always had her Christmas Cactus out on the coffee table and later on, while she was in assisted living, her care givers would tell me that she was always concerned about her plant being watered properly. She would always notice that whenever she had been away for a while the plant would not do as well, but as soon as she was home it would begin to grow again and get new stems and would bloom periodically throughout the year. (A Christmas Cactus is suppose to bloom around the Holiday time usually, unless you give it periods of rest away from the sun and in cool places).

After Grandma passed, nobody knew what to do with the plant. I was afraid to take it because I don't have a green thumb for any plant and I didn't want to be responsible for it dying.

It first bloomed at Christmas that year she passed, which is typical and then it bloomed again on my daughter, Victoria's birthday in March. A bloom showed up then again on my other daughter, Ashley's birthday in June.

I feel that it is somehow connected to her energy. We even call the plant "Grandma" and talk to her all the time. At first I had to remind the kids to take the time to talk with her because she is here.

It just kept growing and growing and blooming and I was afraid to replant her, but I finally decided I needed to. So I transplanted grandma to give her some more breathing room. I used the most expensive soil, and within a few weeks, you could see many new green stems forming. She has grown so much, it is just towering and blooming at very memorable times. Sometimes there were multiple buds, then the buds would split and flower twice. It is amazing that the new buds are there around special days.

It's very comforting to know that our energies are still somehow connected.

Coincidence? Hmm, you know how I feel about that. For the plant to bloom throughout the year without special treatment around special days, I say it's the handy work of a special Angel.

The messages are there. We just have to learn to be aware. They may not happen everyday, and months, maybe years, could go by before you get one. Sometimes it's simply just about asking for a little bit of help. Whether you need some extra strength to get through a rough moment, or when you may be looking for an object like misplaced keys. I misplace things all the time and when I do, I look up and say something as simple as, "Hey

Angels, where did I leave my keys, or where did put the book, etc..." I could use some help finding it. Before I know it, I'm walking in a new direction and I find the item in a place I never would have looked.

These little signs are from your Angels. It's their way of letting you know they are near. They want to help. They can definitely make you smile or bring a tear to your eye. It is reassurance they are with you watching over you.

Chapter 13
CHILDREN & ANGELS

They are like angels, they are God's Children. Like 20:36

Children are fresh, and no, not the sassy type of fresh. Their minds are not filled with earth-like toxins yet of world happenings and life. I was brought up knowing that I was playing with the angels before I was born and other children have said the same. Children love Angels and Angels love children. Their mystery and their beauty, make them feel safe and protected.

There is more of a connection with our young ones and our pets than we realize. We are more in tune to our surroundings when we are young, until the time we are taught to shut it down. "Don't make that stuff up" people say. Who's the imaginary friend your child is playing with? Maybe they are afraid of what others will say or think? Until one day they themselves think that maybe they are just making it up and learn to ignore it, eventually losing touch with the sense of another realm.

The stories that follow will make you believe more than ever that angels ARE real and we CAN communicate with them if only we allow ourselves to do so.

Imaginary Friend as told by Diane S.

Here is a little background to help you better understand the stories that take place next.

I lost a child during pregnancy early on and her name was Rosemary. After the miscarriage, my husband and I were blessed enough to be allowed to adopt a beautiful girl named Delia.

Even as a little baby Delia would look past me, but I never said anything to anyone about it. One day my Mom mentioned to me that Delia would always look over my shoulder and smile. She would look over and above and smile.

When she reached the age of being vocal, one of her first words was TT. She would talk of TT and play with TT quite often. Because she had not been able to say any words as of yet, I really feel like she was trying to say Rosemary.

It started out just in her bedroom. I would always, wonder what she was doing? It just seemed like she was always up always awake. So I would ask her, "what is TT doing?" She really couldn't talk at this time, but she would flap her arms as if she were flapping her wings.

Eventually the interactions would grow into bigger activities and Delia would ask me to participate in things like brushing TT's hair, and I would indulge her request. I would try to join in and play with TT, pretending to brush her hair and Delia would yell at me, "mommy TT's not there she's over there," and then point to another part of the room.

The first time she brought up TT to her father, because I hadn't shared this with anyone yet, it was a little tough since he had lost a lot of faith with the miscarriage experience. I asked him not to take this away from me. Somehow he knew, he believed, and he could feel that this was something real.

Delia would not talk about TT in other areas of the house. Only in her bedroom. Finally at one point TT started to come out of the bedroom and into the living room, into other parts of the home, and eventually outside of the home. Now TT is everywhere, in the car, in the class room. Everyone knows who TT is and they are all comfortable with this.

This Angel is definitely a child. No doubt. There is a picture of me when I was pregnant with my Grandmother. Delia had never met her because she passed before Delia was born. When Delia saw the picture for the first time she immediately knew who it was and what her name was. She said "Ahh there's Gump and there is TT."

Every time she looks at this picture she says that TT is in it. I am pregnant in this picture and there is no way she could know that. TT is not all that she can see. One day she ran into the living room and stopped. Looked at the couch and said "Oh Hi Gump."

So I ask her what does TT look like? Is she itty bitty (because she was tiny when I had her – we called her our little bag of chips). Is she running around, what does she see? She always says that she has red hair. She has recently taken off her wings and has fake wings.

I try so hard to encourage her to continue with these visions. She is so blessed with this gift and I don't want her to lose it.

Diane would like to have deep conversations with Delia, but she is so young, and hopes that one day, Delia, will be able to share much more with her.

When babies look beyond you and giggle, maybe they're seeing angels. ~Quoted in *The Angels' Little Instruction Book* by Eileen Elias Freeman, 1994

How Did You Know? – from Diane S.

Here is another story of an experience of a five year old girl named Shannon. She was with her mom in the grocery store one day when she see's another woman and her cart up ahead. She runs to the woman who was bending over at the time, looks at the cart where the seat is and says, "Oh hi Lauren, How are you?"

The mom of the little girl, caught up with her thinking that the woman's name was Lauren, asked her if she worked at her daughter's school.

Shannon then continues to have a conversation with Lauren and lets her know how beautiful her dress is. She describes the color as she is continuing to talk with Lauren.

Well the woman shopper has now stood up, grabs Shannon by the arm and says, "how do you know my daughter? How do you know what she was buried in?"

There was no visible child in the grocery cart however Shannon had seen this woman's daughter as an Angel.

If you have a child that can see, hear, or play with the angels do not discourage there interactions. Talk with them to help them understand or find someone you can talk to to learn more about it.

Chapter 14
Build It and They Will Come

It is not known precisely where angels dwell — whether in the air, the void, or the planets. It has not been God's pleasure that we should be informed of their abode.
~Voltaire

Ever wonder why good things happen to good people? And some people continually seem to be a magnet for not so good things? You too can better your life with embracing the signs from your Angels. You too can learn to read your signs. Your signs will show up in a format that you will understand. I can not teach you how. It is something you have to learn on your own. I will give you some guidelines of what has worked for me. My other suggestion is to read, read, read, anything you can get your hands on and see how others have been able to acquire strength and guidance from their angels. It has to make sense to you for you.

Maybe you've discussed it with love ones before they have passed.
Maybe someone special collected certain objects likes coins or marbles.
Maybe they are showing you signs in the sky.

Wherever the signs are or whatever their significance is they are there waiting for you to discover. By becoming more aware, being receptive to the idea and asking every day for a sign you will learn how to notice them more. When you do, be sure to thank the universe for every little one you notice.

The signs may be in a pattern or have to be put together like a puzzle but the message will evolve the more you practice.

Start to take a greater notice at the coincidences in your life. Remember my thought that there are no coincidences? Everything happens for a reason. Coincidences are actually a little help from above.

Again, express your gratitude for this gift and learn how to better your spirit with the messages you receive.

You can always show your appreciation by simply being kind to others, offering a smile to someone who appears in need of a loving look, leave a penny for someone to find and bless it with love and happiness.

If you are struggling with finding these signs you may be blocking yourself without even realizing it.

Here are some habits that you can correct to help open the veil and let your angels into your life.

1. You may just plain and simple be afraid. Keep saying I believe, I believe, just like the girl in *The Miracle on 34ᵗʰ Street.*
2. You are too busy in your daily life and do not take a moment to just breath. Find an opportunity even if you are lying in bed at night to just breath.
3. You are trying too hard to see the signs. Just let it happen.
4. Stress and noise can block out the frequency of the energy field trying to get through. Relax in a quiet place. Meditation works for some, burning a candle can give you something to focus on.

5. If you do not listen to the radio then stop hoping for a song through music as a message.
6. Alcohol and drugs will dilute your senses and create a barrier between you and the Angel sphere.
7. You don't believe that you can actually do it.
8. You're afraid your religion will punish you for trying to connect with the spirit world.
9. You don't feel you are deserving of such a gift but you are. Everyone deserves any ounce of happiness that comes their way and any message their angels want to send to you.
10. You're afraid that people will make fun of you. Surprisingly others have jumped onto my bandwagon and enjoy finding the signs, receiving more joy than they could ever imagine.

If you try to omit some of these, or all if you can, you will have a better chance at connecting. I know on the days where I am ramming everywhere, focusing on my new product lines, making sure everything around the house is done, that I do not always see the signs or connect. Then I realize it has been awhile and I focus in a little and then they surprise you again with the littlest of signs.

I have also found that while doing the research for this book and visiting with so many amazing people that I have gained so much more strength with my angels, the signs that appear, and visits from them happen almost on a daily basis!

It goes both ways. If you ignore and do not practice they will not come but if you build your strength and clarity they will come.

Through the years of learning how to connect with my Angels, I have learned so much about myself. It has helped me to become a better person, to appreciate others and what they may be going through.

They have taught me how to love. I mean really, really love. A type of love that can only be from another realm. The type of love that people who have had near death experiences feel when they approach the white light and sense their loved ones who have passed. It's unconditional and unexplainable but you know it when it happens to you.

Unlike the quote above not knowing where our angels are coming from, not yet having the pleasure of being informed....today's society is so much more open to the discussion of each others experiences which in turn is allowing more and more stories to be shared. Believing in these occurrences and being more open to the idea of help from above, I believe God is finally letting us in to this level of frequency.

Showing us a bit more than what we have seen or shared in the past. Who knows what the reasoning is? For so many to have experienced numerous amounts of similar experiences, how can it not be real? Maybe God is showing us this side of our being because of where we are as a whole in society. He's trying to bring us back to a nicer world and show us the meaning of life. Plain and simply – to love one another unconditionally, regardless of race, religion, belief's, etc....

We should be thankful for the gift of life, the chance to breath, to breed, to love..

and in doing so we truly are Never Alone.

About the Author

Michelle Irene Stupski

Michelle is a mother of two children, Derek & Taylor. She has been happily married to her husband, Todd, for over 25 years.

When she was a little girl (around 6), her mother - a dressmaker - started to teach her the art of creating interesting items from fabric. Eventually, with a handbag and a childhood dream of becoming a fashion designer she began designing and making her own handbags in 2004 at her home studio in Binghamton, NY. Thus, MIS Fashion Bags was born

In 2008, Michelle came up with the idea for a convertible and interchangeable handbag system with different bag parts that allow you to style, create, and restyle the perfect bag for you!

The first design is actually named after her mother, Margarete, who was such an inspiration in her life.

The design was created while her Mom was battling cancer for the 4th time and, "I remember bringing the bag during one of her chemo treatments to get her thoughts. We would sit there for hours and it gave us something positive to focus on." says Michelle

The collection allows you to mix and match the interchangeable components to create a look you love. Then, when the mood strikes or the need for some different features arise, you can restyle it with ease. Now you can put your personal stamp on your ensemble and carry the perfect bag for any occasion!

Michelle Irene is a brand division of her company MIS Fashion Bags and now, with the publication of this book a new brand division is born: *The Never Alone Angel Line* by Michelle Irene

- This includes inspirational jewelry that can be personalized after that special someone in your life who gives you strength, courage or a special loved one whom has passed on that taught you much about life.

- The new Spirit Spritzer line, made of 100% essential oil can be used as room freshener, body spray, relaxation, mediation, etc...

- A line of Angel Inspiration Cards for daily reassurance that you are Never Alone in any situation in life and to guide you in living the greatly enriched life that you deserve.

- Angel Coins/Charms to help guide you and inspire you everyday or when the time is needed.

You can find these products and more at:

www.michelleirene.com   www.neveraloneangels.com

The links for Facebook, Twitter and Pinterest are available at these sites so come follow me on this amazing journey!